HOW TO USE A COMPASS FOR KIDS

A Beginners' Guide to Land
Navigation, Fun Compass Games,
and Activities

by

Graham Rick Grey

Climax Publishers

A FREE GIFT TO OUR READERS!

Guidelines to Teach Self-Control to Kids

Get FREE, unlimited access to it

and all our new books by Joining our community!

CONTENTS

CHAPTER 1 : INTRODUCTION

1.1 Compass

A compass is a tool that points out cardinal directions, such as North, South, East, and West. In more detail, it is a magnetized piece of metal that orients itself towards the Earth's magnetic North Pole. This invaluable tool has been used for centuries to help guide travelers and adventurers to their desired destinations.

Fig.1: A Compass

1.2 How Does a Compass Work?

The Earth is a massive magnet with two points of force: the North and South Poles. As the planet rotates, its core, primarily molten iron, generates a magnetic field. This creates the north and south magnetic poles and allows compasses to function. The needle in a compass is made of magnetized metal, usually iron, and is suspended in liquid (usually mineral oil or white spirit) so that it can freely turn.

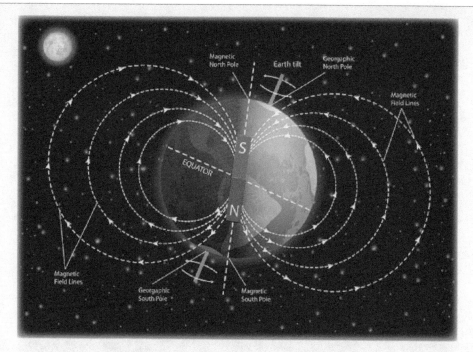

Fig.2: Earth's Magnetic Field

The compass needle detects the Earth's magnetic field and points to Magnetic North when the held level is in the palm. The user of the gadget can then determine the remaining directions.

In addition, there are little measurements all around the Compass. These are referred to as degrees. The red end of the needle always points north, while the white/black endpoints south. On the outside cover of the Compass is a top arrow referred to as the 'orientation arrow.

1.3 What Is the Purpose of a Compass?

The Compass enabled the creation of maps and even helped to demonstrate that the Earth is a sphere, not a flat plane. Without any landmarks to aid navigation, compasses were primarily used by sailors at sea. They relied on the stars, particularly Polaris, the North Star, to guide them. When the weather was gloomy, rainy, or foggy, the sailors could not determine their direction without a compass, making it an invaluable tool for seafaring.

Fig 3: A ship in a stormy sea

1.4 The History of The Compasses
Before Magnetic Compass

Before the creation of the Compass, navigation primarily relied on astronomy and the position of the sun and stars, a practice known as celestial navigation. To provide directions during their journey, sailors would use landmarks and terrain to get their bearings, either by cruising close to landmasses to get a sense of their location or by relying on celestial navigation when traversing vast oceans or seas.

Discovery of Magnetic Compass

Around 200 BC, the Chinese Han and Tang Dynasties were the first to utilize a compass. They realized that certain naturally magnetic metals from the Earth could be used to magnetize iron needles in the early varieties of the Compass. This metal was known as lodestone or magnetite. Magnets were employed in spiritual ways in non-European nations, such as divination, geomancy, and Feng Shui, to assist in optimizing good fortune.

In the early days of compasses, the magnetic needle was affixed to a wood piece that drifted in a water dish. These were mainly utilized as backups when the sun or stars were not visible in the sky. The tools became increasingly popular and helpful, and more and more people learned to use them.

As early scientists learned more about magnetism in the 12th century, the compass needle was mounted on a pin, and compass cards were added in the 13th century. This compass card initially displayed the four cardinal directions, but the design grew to include 32 directional points over time. Compass and charts were widely employed by sailing ships in the 16th century.

1.5 Essential Compass Vocabulary

Let's go through some popular navigation phrases shortly.

True North:

The Earth's physical north pole. (Fig.2)

Magnetic North:

The magnet needle points to the magnetic North following the ever-changing Earth's magnetic field. (Fig.2)

This direction indicates the top of your map. However, it is a line rather than a single point.

Declination:

Declination is the difference in the number of degrees between true North and magnetic North. (Fig.2). The angle fluctuates based on your location and progressively shifts as the planet's tectonic plates move.

An agonic line is an imaginary line that passes through the North Pole and North Magnetic Pole, represented by points on the Earth's surface at which magnetic north and true north coincide. Agonic, meaning "lacking an angle," refers to the lines along which the declination angle is zero. This line is of particular importance to navigators, as it allows them to determine their position on the globe accurately.

In the USA, the agonic line, also known as the zero-declination line, passes through central Wisconsin. So, in Wisconsin, the declination is close or at zero degrees, making Compass use easy. But if you are east or west of the agonic line, you must account for the difference to receive appropriate instructions from the map to the field or vice versa. The greater the declination, the greater the distance from the agonic line; you will need to add or subtract several degrees to acquire an exact bearing.

Examine maps to determine the declination in the given

location. Because the magnetic pole constantly shifts, declination may vary slightly from year to year. Thus it is recommended to utilize maps that are recently dated.

Bearing:

A bearing is the direction of an object (such as a campsite, a mountain, or your goal) relative to your current location. Bearings are measured in degrees from 0 (North) to 360 (South).

Compass Rose:

A compass rose is a sign that appears on nautical charts, compasses, and maps. It is also known as the rose of the winds, the wind rose, or the compass star.

The Compass rose was created by Europeans in the 12th century. It permitted the construction of the eight principal winds, consisting of the four cardinal and new inter-cardinal directions. The significant winds are the Polar Easterlies, the Prevailing Westerlies, and the Trade Winds. Each one of them rules roughly 30 degrees of latitude. It is like the wind moves in circles around the Earth.

Figure 4: Compass Rose

CHAPTER 2 :
ANATOMY OF
COMPASS

Before you can go through the most perplexing wilderness and yet find your way back home, you must first understand what that piece of plastic and magnetic magic in your palm is.

A good exploration compass will contain the following features:

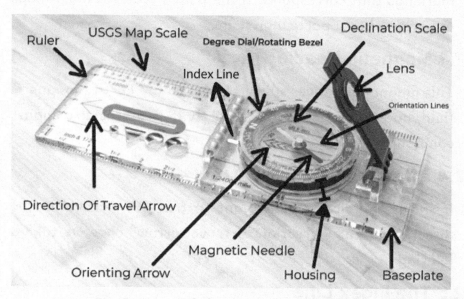

Fig:5. Parts of the Baseplate Compass

2.1 Baseplate

This flat, often rectangular surface contains the Compass and is labeled with lines, numbers, and other information required to convert map data into information that can be utilized in the actual world. Users may view the map via transparent baseplates. Compasses of the highest quality will be made to fit their users' palms comfortably.

2.2 Rulers and Scales

Circling the circumference of the baseplate, these lines and numerals reflect paper lengths and interpretation of actual distances. Hikers use the baseplate's straight edge, measured as a straight line, to depict the distance between two places on a map. Examine the baseplate edge of a compass for markings that correspond to the issue's scale, as most maps are created to a particular scale.

2.3 Magnetic Needle

This magnetized sliver spins relative to the Earth's magnetic field, and its red end points north. It is a crucial compass component.

2.4 Direction of Travel Arrow

It shows the direction we want to travel. We travel in the direction of the "direction of travel arrow" once we take a bearing.

2.5 The Index Line

The Index Line is a fixed line within the compass housing, aligned with the direction of travel arrow. The index line marks the bearing you set by rotating the bezel.

2.6 Orienting Arrow

This is a case-mounted directing arrow that is fixed on the dial and aligned with North on housing. It may be aligned with the red end of the magnetic needle and held there in orienteering to guarantee that a hiker follows the correct bearing. It is then called "Red is in the Shed."

2.7 An Important Concept: Red is in the Shed

"Red is in the shed" means that the red-painted side of the magnetic needle is precisely aligned with the orienting arrow. It will be further elaborated in the coming text. (Fig.5)

2.8 Magnifier/Lens

A magnifying glass allows the observer to zoom in on certain map information. Like a tiny party hat on a spherical head, the magnifier could be attached to the direction of the travel arrow.

2.9 Dial

This rotating circle encompasses the compass housing. A full circle is measured in degrees, from o to 360 degrees.

2.10 Declination Scale

The Declination Scale on a map is a line or set of lines that indicate the difference between True North and Magnetic North in degrees. The Declination Scale is a vital tool for measuring and plotting bearings. It is typically found on the edge of a map and marked with an angle and the angular difference's Direction (E or W). It differs based on the user's position worldwide. Declination swings throughout time and varies from year to year.

2.11 Orientation Lines

These lines go parallel to the arrow of orientation and rotate with it. Mainly when put on a map, they aid in navigating.

2.12 Housing

This box, which is elevated above the remainder of the baseplate, contains the spinning needle. The dial is its pivot point.

Important Message:

Every Compass Is Unique. Some have everything mentioned here, while others include mirrors and other features for more advanced techniques, yet others are stripped-down tools ideal for learning the fundamentals. The Compass Jargon May Appear Confusing at First, But Trust Us: You'll Pick It Up Quickly, Especially If You Practice In The Wild. With the assistance of an experienced friend, just in case.

CHAPTER 3 : COMPASS DIRECTIONS

A compass is an essential tool for map readers. It indicates which direction is north and east, south and west. These are four cardinal points. Typically, the north side of a map is created, pointing upward.

3.1 Four Types Of North

Four popular north definitions:

1. Magnetic North

The direction a magnetic compass will point in. A magnetic compass will always display magnetic North; however, depending on where you are in the nation and the date of your visit, there will be a variation between magnetic north and grid north, as stated on your map key.

2. Grid North

It is the orientation of the vertical map grid lines. It differs very little from the true North.

3. True North

It is the direction leading to Earth's Geographic North Pole

4. Assumed North

It is the assumed north during a survey. It changes from survey to survey.

3.2 Cardinal Directions

A Bearing gives us direction. The four principal directions are:

North (N),

South (S),

East (E), and

West (W).

These are called Cardinal Directions.

If you see your Compass clockwise, they are NESW; each arrives at ninety degrees from the next.

3.3 Ordinal Directions

The Ordinal directions, also called inter-cardinal directions, are created by a line in-between each cardinal point. These directions are:

Northeast (NE)

Southeast (SE)

Southwest (SW), and

Northwest (NW).

For Example, North-East is located among the North and the East (NE).

These are shown in Following Image.

Fig 6: Cardinal and Inter-Cardinal Directions

3.4 Secondary Inter-Cardinal Directions

Sometimes an additional 8 points for a total of sixteen directions are used.

Every one of these points in a different direction. The west-southwest (WSW) direction is west of the southwest. North-northeast (NNE) is the direction to the North of the northeast.

North–North–East is denoted as NNE.

East–North–East is denoted as ENE.

East–South–East is characterized as ESE.

South–South–East is indicated as SSE

South–South–West is marked as SSW.

West–South–West is marked as WSW.

West–North–West is represented as WNW.

North–North–West is defined as NNW.

Fig 7: An Image depicting Sixteen Directions

CHAPTER 4 : TYPES OF COMPASSES

4.1 Magnetic compass

The most ubiquitous type of Compass is the magnetic Compass, which is used to ascertain the direction of magnetic North. This Compass is constructed by affixing a magnetized piece of iron or steel to a low-friction base, allowing it to rotate freely. To make it easier to identify the north direction, the northern end of the metal piece is usually painted red, allowing the other directions to be determined easily. It has the following types:

Fig 8: Compass displayed against pebbles

Lensatic Compass or Prismatic Compass

The prismatic or lensatic Compass is one of several types of Compasses.

A hairline cover and a glass prism or lens are included in a prismatic compass. On the other hand, this Compass is equipped with a ruler and magnifying lens for map reading, a light for poor light circumstances. It is typically employed in military or intelligence operations.

A prismatic compass is a surveyor's hand compass equipped with peep sights and a triangular glass prism, enabling the user to view the magnetic bearing. This sophisticated tool is essential for surveyors, providing them with an accurate and reliable way to measure direction.

Fig 9: Lensatic Military Compass

Compass for Surveyors

The surveyor's Compass is one of the most common varieties of compasses. Surveyors use it to determine the magnetic bearing of a line of sight and to measure horizontal angles.

Base Plate Compass

A base plate compass is a compass with a clear, rectangular plastic base filled with liquid. It is also known as an Orienteering compass.

Fig 10: A Base Plate Compass

Thumb Compasses

A thumb compass is more straightforward and smaller than a base plate compass, making it ideal for trail runners and hikers. As its name suggests, it hooks the user's thumb and takes up little room in a hydration pack. It is less sophisticated than a base plate compass but helps with map orientation.

Solid-State Compass

These various types of Compasses, which can be found in digital clocks, mobile phones, and tablets, are gaining popularity among seagoing vessels. Magnetic field sensors input the device's orientation into a microcontroller.

Liquid Compass

The liquid Compass is one of the many types of Compass used today. A magnetic needle or dial and a compass card are positioned on a pivot within a liquid-filled capsule in this type of Compass.

Common liquids include mineral oil, lamp oil, ethyl alcohol, white spirits, and refined kerosene.

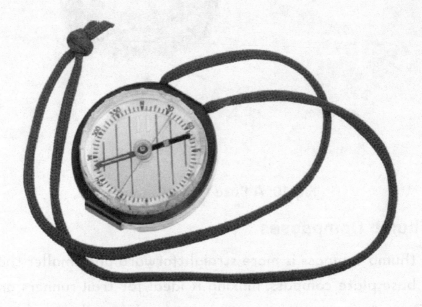

Fig 11: Liquid Compass

4.2 Astro Compass

The Astro compass is one of the distinct types of Compasses. An astrocompass utilizes the positions of many celestial planets to calculate true North. This instrument is deployed in polar locations where magnetic compasses and gyrocompasses are unreliable.

4.3 Gyroscope

A gyrocompass employs an electrically driven, quicker gyroscope wheel and frictional forces to compute true North using the rules of physics, the influence of gravity, and the Earth's rotation, among other factors.

4.4 GPS Compass

Its full name is the Global Positioning System. A GPS compass employs satellites in geosynchronous orbit around the Earth to pinpoint the exact location and direction of the bearer's movement.

CHAPTER 5 : HOW TO SELECT A COMPASS

A compass and a map are essential for anyone exploring unfamiliar territory. A compass ensures navigation to your bearing and stays stable due to external factors such as weather. At the same time, maps provide accurate visual representations of key landmarks, helping travelers orient themselves. When choosing a compass, there are four key considerations:

1. Declination Adjustments:

It should be possible for hikers and other path users to adjust the declination of their Compass.

Since declination varies depending on location, variable declination is essential. You set it and forget it with adjustable declination till you travel to a different place.

2. Sighting Mirror:

Consider upgrading to a model of sighting mirror along with declination adjustment and this functionality if you want to travel off-trail or demand more precise navigation.

3. Clinometer:

A clinometer on a compass can assist you in identifying avalanche threats while mountaineering or backcountry skiing. A clinometer is also helpful for field scientists and search-and-rescue personnel.

4. Global needle:

Obtain a model with a worldwide hand if you are a world traveler. This feature compensates for differences in the magnetic field, allowing a compass to perform smoothly and precisely worldwide. A compass is otherwise either for North or South America.

Be Cautious

Replica compasses on keychains, watchbands, and zipper pulls are funny but ineffective navigational tools. A Compass feature on a multi-function watch cannot replace a simple needle-style baseplate compass.

CHAPTER 6 : NAVIGATION

Navigation comes from the Latin words Navis (ship) and agere (steer) ("to drive"). Navigation determines a ship's position and distance traveled. Navigation avoids crashes, saves fuel, and meets time limits.

To do better navigation, you need to understand several types of maps.

6.1 Types of Maps

Part of the appeal of maps is that they can be used for everything from navigating to establishing ownership to displaying information. Please continue reading to learn about various map types and their applicability. In reference to ICSM (Intergovernmental Committee on Surveying and Mapping), five maps are below.

1. General Reference Maps

Fig 12: An Example of Reference Map

General reference maps are a fantastic way to get a basic understanding of the geography of an area. These maps usually include important landmarks and political boundaries, but they may provide less detail than other maps. They cover cities, towns, significant transit lines, and natural features such as lakes and rivers. General reference maps can be found online and in print form. They are helpful for quickly gaining an overview of an area, but they are unsuitable for navigation or in-depth exploration.

2. Topographical Maps

Fig 13: An Example of Topographical Map

Topographical maps include contour lines to show the elevation of the terrain and may also show human-made features such as roads, buildings, and boundaries. They are often used for navigation, planning, or military operations.

3. Thematic Maps

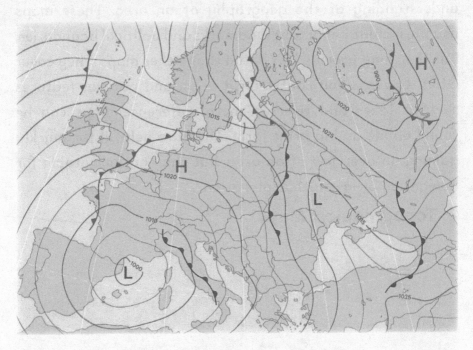

Fig 14: Weather Forcast Map

The purpose of thematic maps is to showcase information on specific themes instead of charting the surrounding area or indicating where to go. Thematic maps have been used to follow whale migrations, and they may depict anything from geology to population density to weather.

4. Navigational Charts

In addition to general reference and topographical maps, nautical charts are indispensable for sea or air navigation. They provide vital information for avoiding disasters, such as the location of underwater rocks and any specialized navigation devices.

Fig 15: A Navigational Map Along with Hand Magnifier.

5. Cadastral Maps and Plans

Cadastral maps, also called Naksha, are digital land records. Cadastral mapping is one of the earliest types of mapping; when the Nile flooded, the ancient Egyptians developed cadastral records to determine property ownership.

Cadastral maps are far more detailed, and, despite their widespread usage, you will not meet one every day. When a structure or parcel of land is surveyed, the resulting plans illustrate individual properties, including boundary information. They may be incorporated to create much larger cadastral maps.

Fig 16: An Example of a Cadastral Map

CHAPTER 7 : HOW TO USE A COMPASS

7.1 Steps for Reaching a Safety Bearing:

Before operating a compass, it is essential to understand its components, so please review them again. To ensure that you are secure in the wilderness, select a landmark in the distance that will guide you to a safe location. This could be a tree, a hilltop, a road you previously identified on a map, or any other recognizable feature. This is known as a safety bearing, and if you ever find yourself lost, you can use it to reach safety. For example, let's say the safety bearing is a road located to the west, and whenever you are lost, you can follow this bearing to safety.

Step 1 : Hold the Compass Properly

1. Hold it with the palm up.

2. The direction of the travel arrow facing forward

3. Keep your arms fixed. Please keep it away from all metals because any metal or magnet near the needle may throw off your bearings.

Fig 17: Holding Compass Properly

Step 2 : Dial it in

Hold the compass firm and level as you rotate the bezel until the West mark on the bezel and the index line align.

Fig 18: Dialing the Compass

Step 3 : Red is in the Shed and Finding the Bearing

Now, as explained before, while holding the Compass, start rotating your body until the red is in the shed. This will be your direction of travel. We can now accurately read the bearing at the point where the Direction of Travel Arrow intersects the dial. For e.g., it is 240 degrees, as shown in the figure.

Red is in the shed means that the red color painted side of the needle is precisely in line and within the orienting arrow.

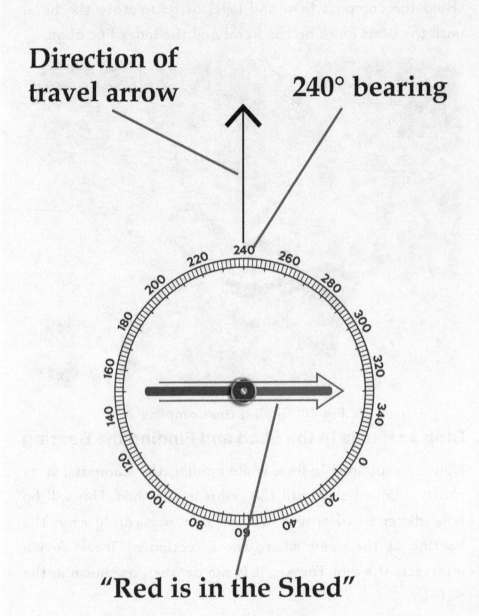

Direction of travel arrow

240° bearing

"Red is in the Shed"

Fig 19: Red is in the shed

7.2 How to Use a Map and a Compass
Step 1

Place the map on a level and flat surface.

To begin, you must locate yourself on the map and mark it with a cross or dot.

Fig 20: Hold the map Flat

Step 2

Also, mark the destination on the map with a cross or dot.

Step 3

Now, join the two dots in a straight line, and it will show you the path you have to follow to reach the destination.

Step 4

Take the baseplate compass and place its direction of travel arrow along that line.

Step 5

Start rotating the dial to align the orientation lines with the grid lines that run on the map.

Fig 21: Orienteering using a map and Compass

Step 6

Account for the declination angle.

Declination varies from place to place. In the United Kingdom, magnetic changes are negligible (a few degrees) and are typically overlooked. In the continental United States, declination runs from 20 degrees east in portions of Washington to 20 degrees west in parts of Maine. Because a one-degree error might generate an error of 100 feet across a mile, it is essential to account for declination accurately.

To fix declination, you must figure out what it is in your route location. Most maps have a legend at the bottom that shows the zone's declination. Keep in mind that the decline of specific places changes over time, so check the date on the map.

The "Magnetic Declination Calculator" from NOAA (National Oceanic and Atmospheric Administration) will assist you in determining acceptable declination values.

Depending on the magnitude of declination in your travel zone, you must either ADD positive magnetic variation or SUBTRACT negative variation.

For instance, New York's declination is -12°. Three hundred sixty degrees minus 12° degrees equals 348 degrees.

Step 7: Finding the Bearing:

Hold the Compass in front of you and start rotating your body till the red is in the shed. At that very point, it will show you the direction of travel. We can now accurately read the bearing at the point where the Direction of Travel Arrow intersects the dial. Again, red in the shed means that the red color painted side of the needle is precisely in line and within the orienting arrow.

Fig 22: Finding the bearing

7.3 Using a Compass and a Map to Determine Your Location: Triangulation

Step 1

Find an area or a ridge with good visibility; ideally, 360 degrees of surroundings are visible.

Step 2

Place your map flat on the ground surface and orient it to the North. For that, place the Compass flat on the map. Rotate the map until the grid lines are aligned with the compass needle. The map should now be oriented to the terrain.

Please remember that depending on your location, you may need to adjust for declination. To compensate, repeat Step number Six from the 7.2 'How to Use a Map and a Compass'.

Fig 23: Place the Map on the Flat Ground

Step 3

Identify a landmark visually, say, a hill, and point the direction of travel arrow of your Compass towards it. Start rotating the bezel until red is in the shed.

Step 4

Now, coming down to the map, put the tip of the Compass on the hill labeled on the map, rotate the whole Compass, not the bezel, till the red is in the shed, and draw a line on the map.

Fig 24: Drawing a Line on the Map

Step 5

Repeat steps 3 & 4 with a second and third landmark at an angle of at least 60 degrees from the first landmark.

Step 6

Draw the three lines, and your location is determined by where your drawn lines intersect. If the three red lines make a small triangle, your position will be within or near it. If the lines create a vast triangle, you should double-check your work since you nearly committed an error.

> **Free Triangulation:**
>
> If you already have one point of reference, such as a trail you are hiking on, you only need to take one field bearing to determine your location. This technique, known as free triangulation, involves plotting the bearing on a map and noting where it intersects the trail. By doing so, you can quickly identify your current position.

7.4 Using a Compass for kids: Camping Areas

Family camping excursions are an excellent opportunity to teach your children essential life lessons such as cooking, exploring, survival skills, and much more.

Fig 25: A Robo Scout

A solid sense of direction is one of the most critical skills you can tutor your child from an early age. If they lose their sense of direction, they will feel more at ease and confident that they will be able to find their way back to their starting position. And, let's face it, whether we like to admit it or not, we all get lost from time to time! Certain things we may teach our children about direction, like the sun rising in the east and falling in the west, will benefit them in their life.

Fig 26: Tutoring a child is an investment in our future

But what if the sky is overcast?

As a result, the Compass is unquestionably the most helpful instrument we have at our disposal. Using one may be enjoyable and valuable, especially once we've learned the fundamentals. Knowing which way you're looking and which direction you wish to go is a talent you may utilize every day without even recognizing it.

How to use a compass as a kid

To minimize information overload and misunderstanding, teach a youngster to use a compass in modest, fundamental steps. Begin by showing them the four cardinal directions: North, east, west, and south.

How Can We Remember?

"Not Eat Shredded Wheat"

You undoubtedly remember the acronym you were given as a child and giving them one to memorize can help them recall the guidelines.

Here are a handful of such examples:

Not Eat Shredded Wheat   Nor Eat Soggy Waffles

Anything enjoyable and easy to remember will keep your children entertained, so have some fun with it and try to make up your own if you want.

Learning the 4 Cardinal Directions with a Compass for Kids

Only remembering the acronym is half the fight. Children must understand that each letter signifies a different direction. Try having them point forward while indicating north. Then, instruct them to make a quarter turn clockwise and face east. Another quarter turns to the south, followed by another quarter to the west.

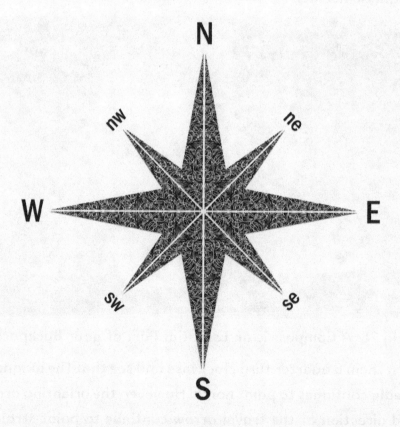

Fig 27: A Compass Rose showing eight directions.

Once they have mastered the fundamentals, it's time to hit outdoors.

Holding a Compass

Request that they hold it flat and away from their body. Emphasize that the arrow will always point north. This will assist kids in learning and remembering that the needle indicates North.

You may then begin to show them how to establish their bearing so they can follow a path. Permit them to rotate the dial and line the orientation arrow with the Compass's magnetic needle.

Fig 28: A Compass is an Essential Part of your Backpack.

Turn them a quarter turn clockwise and see that the magnetic needle continues to point north! However, the orienting arrow and direction of the travel arrow continue to point straight out in front of their body.

Allow them to spin the dial to re-align the orienting arrow

with the magnetic needle. The journey arrow points east, but the magnetic and orienting are heading north. Explain that following the direction of the travel arrow will lead them eastward. Allow your kid to walk about straight for a few minutes.

Once they've mastered it, have them spin around and try to regain their bearings—this time in a different direction.

Make Using a Compass Exciting

Making a game out of it will be both entertaining and educational. Make it more interesting by putting various things about the yard for kids to uncover as they follow bearings to specific areas. Primarily, make it light and enjoyable! Your youngster will quickly learn to use the Compass!

CHAPTER 8 : THE GLOBAL POSITIONING SYSTEM (GPS)

Since compasses and maps have been used for navigation for thousands of years, GPS gadgets are a comparatively recent navigation technology. After years of military usage, the government released GPS satellites in the 1980s for civilian use.

Two times every day, a network of 24 satellites circles the Earth and transmits signals back to it. A GPS receiver detects a user's location by collecting signals from at least three satellites. Determine when a satellite sends and when your system gets a call. After Combining data from many broadcasts, the receiver calculates the user's location. It also tells you your journey speed and the time required to reach your destination. Numerous GPS devices have an accuracy of 50 feet or less (15 meters).

Multiple GPS systems include satellite signal information in their maps. Depending on your chosen GPS unit, your device may have road, marine, topographic, trail, and ski resort maps. Remember that GPS devices may be used when driving, cycling, running, exercising, boating, fishing, flying, and hiking. If your smartphone lacks the needed maps, you can purchase and download them individually. Map prices vary substantially. Some maps (such as those of national parks) are available online, whereas device-specific maps cost more.

You may have used a GPS while driving. The gadget calculates a route and a route back home when an address is supplied. Many systems will also integrate issues around traffic and development. But how can a GPS help with navigating in the wilderness?

8.1 GPS Navigation

A GPS receiver displays your location, distance, direction, paths, and tracking information. If you monitor your GPS device, it will leave a breadcrumb trail so you can retrace your steps. Before using a GPS device, it must be initialized and configured. It is necessary to get a signal from the satellites. You should only use the device for navigation if signals are strong and the system can locate sufficient satellites. Clear skies are ideal for transmitting a powerful movement. This might be hard if you are in a dense forest canopy.

Use coordinates from your map to program your GPS gadget. Establish waypoints along the route from where you parked your vehicle to where you pitch your tent. Your Course will be constructed using these waypoints. This information is available in the device's instruction manual. You must be able to read a map. Before venturing into a new place with your GPS gadget, practice at home. The local outdoor supply store may provide classes on using GPS devices and fundamental navigational skills.

Never put your life in a battery.

Realizing the importance of a map and compass in addition to a GPS device is essential. Unlike a GPS device, the batteries in a compass and the signal on a map will never die, making them reliable. Also, according to experts, the USGS Topographic Maps are the most accurate and frequently updated. Consider your GPS device a helpful companion to your compass and maps, but Please remember that a GPS unit's effectiveness largely depends on the map used in it.

8.2 Compass VS GPS

To decide which is better, a compass or a GPS, we must consider the advantages and disadvantages of each. First, consider Compass's advantages and disadvantages.

Compass Pros:

It's a little, pocket-sized gadget that's ideal for when you need to travel light.

It is reasonably priced.

It does not require any power to function. It comes out of the package and is ready to use.

A compass is so essential that you can create one with items you already have at home.

Fig 29: A GPS Navigation System Vs. A Compass

Compass cons:

To correctly read a compass, you must acquire a skill

Most individuals recognize the need for a compass, but do they all realize how to operate one?

A compass can only show you north if you don't have a map. Your Compass may be useless if you're utterly lost and have yet to learn where you are.

Let us Check GPS Pros & Cons:

GPS Pros:

Many maps may fit in the palm of your hand. On a map, the device will locate your specific position. On the go, an electronic compass is more convenient than a conventional compass. The GPS device will inform you how far you've traveled and how far you still need to travel. It can also provide altitude.

GPS Cons:

All GPS gadgets operate on electric batteries. What happens if the supplies are off? Extras are usually appreciated, but they add to your load. A GPS unit is an electrical equipment that can be damaged or rendered inoperable if dropped or exposed to water.

For proper operation, a strong signal is necessary. Most buildings, tunnels, dense forest canopies, and cloudy days will not receive a signal.

Finally, a GPS device may give more comprehensive navigational data than a compass. But, because it is battery-operated and requires a reliable internet connection, every hiker should always carry a compass and map.

CHAPTER 9 : FUN COMPASS GAMES AND ACTIVITIES

These compass games teach kids how to operate the Compass. How to use a compass is an essential skill for any outdoor lover, but it is not just for adventurous adults. Teaching youngsters compass skills is a fantastic technique to help them build their abstract reasoning and visual problem-solving abilities.

Making compass activities that require kids to use their Compass is a beautiful technique for teaching these abilities to your children. Here are a few recommendations:

9.1 COMPASS WALK
Materials:

Each kid receives a compass and individually wrapped candy.

Method:

A candy is set on the ground in an ample open space. The kid must stand where the candy is, set their Compass to 360 degrees, face north, and take fifty steps. They then put their Compass to 120 degrees and walk 50 steps in that direction before repeating. Finally, they put their Compass to a bearing of 240 degrees and proceeded 50 paces. When they are done, they may pick up the candy, place it in their pocket, or consume it if they are within five feet.

It is excellent if the candy is buried in the grass so that the kid does not find it until the final leg of the triangle has been completed.

Variation 1:

The kid adds 120 degrees to the first and second bearings when determining bearings.

Variation 2:

Kids create a triangle while carrying paper grocery bags on their heads.

9.2 Compass Ball

This game will assist young children in learning the cardinal directions. For this activity, you will require a basketball court, a basketball, and a way of marking court regions, e.g., Markers, chalks, etc.

Fig 30: Compass Ball

Mark eight positions on the court, one for each cardinal and ordinal direction, with North beneath the basket and south at the 3-point arc's center.

At the start, divide the participants into two teams. The teams will take turns shooting the ball until each player has gone the agreed-upon number of times (the number of turns should be scaled to the size of your group and the amount of time available).

You will yell out one of the eight cardinal or ordinal directions when starting each round. The teammate whose turn it is must instantly reach the target area and throw the ball. If a team member gets to the wrong end, they cannot shoot. If a teammate goes to the correct location, they will receive two points and be allowed to shoot. If a teammate makes a basket, they will receive an extra issue.

After each player has taken the agreed-upon number of turns, total each team's score. The team with the most points emerges triumphant.

9.3 Closed Course

This compass game may be adjusted for students with varied degrees of familiarity. Each team will need a compass, a place marker, and a direction sheet for this game.

Divide your party into three teams of three members each.

Ensure that your instructions document will take your teams back to where they started. This is how you'll know whether they did everything correctly.

You may adjust your child's direction sheet to their ability level by utilizing simply cardinal directions for beginners, cardinal and ordinal directions for intermediate difficulties, and bearings for more experienced youngsters, as previously indicated.

A simple (Cardinal Points Only) game works like this:

Take five steps south.

Take ten steps east.

Take 20 steps northward.

Take 15 steps westward.

Move your feet 15 steps to the south.

Take 5 steps eastward.

Whereas more advanced game (Using Bearings) looks something like this:

Turn 180 degrees and walk 20 steps in that direction.

Take a 45-degree heading and walk in that direction for 28 steps.

Take a 315-degree bearing and walk in that direction for 28 steps.

Take 28 steps in the direction indicated by a bearing of 22 degrees.

Take a 90-degree turn, then 28 steps in that direction.

9.4 The game of trial swap

This game allows your children to construct their navigation routes and perform the courses designed by their classmates. For each team, you will need two small place markers that can't be seen from afar (golf trees work well), a compass, a pen, and paper.

Distribute the teams after dividing the group into three. Place one of each team's markers at the start of their path, then write a set of instructions for them to follow and place the second marker where the instructions lead.

Allow the teams to exchange directions and follow each other's path. The game ends after all the groups have finished all the courses.

An interesting twist is to play the Trail Swap Game at night or in a dark gymnasium with spotlights.

CHAPTER 10 : TIPS, TRICKS, AND FACTS

Navigating with a compass doesn't have to be intimidating or confusing! With the correct information and some practice, anyone can quickly become an expert at using a compass. When using a compass to navigate, there are a few things to remember.

10.1 Tips and Tricks

The first tip is to remember to adjust the declination angle whenever entering new coordinates. Otherwise you might take a few wrong turns!It is preferable to break the travel into tiny chunks while keeping a bearing towards distant things in mind.

You may also check your bearing at intervals to verify that you're on the correct road. This is especially significant in untamed terrains such as woods or high-altitude locations.

Aim your Compass away from ferrous items. This may be the buckle on your belt or a survival machete on your hip. Spreading the map and using the Compass on the bonnet of a car can also throw you off. Aside from that, electrical wires can interfere with compass readings. It is essential to be aware of your surroundings before utilizing a compass.

Try to maintain the Compass as level as possible when taking a heading. This will increase the accuracy of the readings.

Practice using the Compass in your neighborhood before venturing into the field. Through training, you will become flawless.

Even if you don't have a map, a compass can help you find your way north in an emergency. This might also assist you in reorienting yourself if you are lost.

Keep a magnetic compass away from laptops, cell phones, and pocket radios.

10.2 Interesting Compass Facts

Here are some intriguing compass facts for you to consider.

Hundreds of years after its invention, the Compass was utilized for divination.

The Chinese compass "south-pointing spoon," which pointed south, was among the first compass designs.

There are 32 points on the Western Compass where the rose-of-winds may be found. While Eastern has 48. Ancient Arab compasses had 32 points as well. These days, compasses are marked with degrees instead of cardinal points

Boxing the Compass refers to identifying all 32 points of the Compass, beginning with The North, in a clockwise direction.

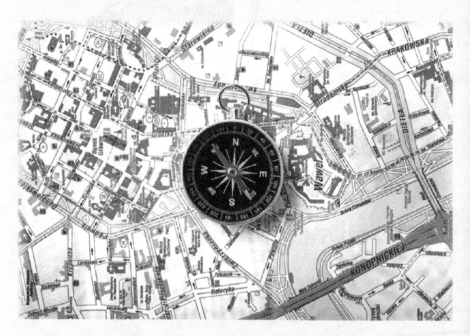

Fig 31: Compass placed on the map

Nearby ferrous objects or electromagnetic fields influence compasses; hence, they must be corrected and calibrated when used on metal-laden vessels, such as boats or airplanes. This is accomplished by inserting magnets into the housing of the Compass.

Compasses were smuggled into German POW camps during World War II to aid in their escape, disguised as buttons and razor blades.

The first time the Chinese used a compass for navigation compared to divination was a floating magnetic needle in a water bowl.

A Qibla compass, sometimes called a Qibla compass, is a sort of Compass utilized by Muslims to determine the direction to face when praying in Makkah.

Fig 32: Qibla Direction

Rose-of-winds are frequently printed in low-light-visibility colors on maps. Typically, the compass rose represents the eight principal points of the Compass in black. Typically, quarter-wind points are red, whereas half-wind points are blue or green.

10.5 Smartphone as Compass

You can use a digital compass app on your smartphone since it has a magnetometer. You may select from many apps accessible in the app stores.

Fig 33: Compass in SmartPhone

Electromagnetic fields, electrical devices, and metallic objects can all affect the accuracy of digital compasses. As such, it is essential to regularly calibrate the compass to ensure accuracy. On iOS devices, you can enable compass calibration by going to Location Services. For Android devices, after launching the compass app, you can increase the accuracy of the compass by moving the phone in a figure-eight pattern.

A smartphone compass does not provide the standard

direction of travel arrows and orienteering lines. However, an iOS compass may be used to navigate using Apple Maps. You may use the inbuilt Compass in Google Maps to calculate your journey direction. The Compass, on the other hand, will be limited by the capabilities of the smartphone battery. Furthermore, you must rely on sources other than cell phone signals for navigation in the bush.

Smartphones come with a compass app already installed. This app will use the phone's built-in sensors to detect the direction you are pointing in.

CONCLUSION

I extend my sincere good wishes for a safe and prosperous expedition as you embark on your outdoor adventures. It is essential to exercise caution, be aware of your surroundings, and plan to ensure the best possible experience. Consider researching current weather and trail conditions before departure, stocking up on essentials such as food, water, and first aid supplies, and familiarizing yourself with local regulations. Additionally, make sure you document your journey, as it can provide documentation in an emergency. I hope that this brief advice helps enhance the joy of your trip - again, all the best luck on your journey.

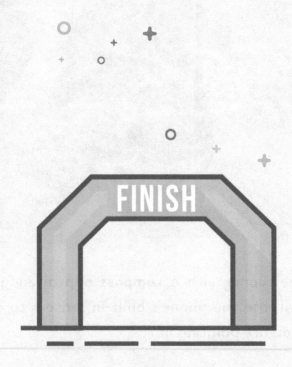

Made in the USA
Coppell, TX
05 October 2023

22465169R00046